Careers

371.425
FIR

Helping Hands

At the Fire Station

Ruth Thomson

WAYLAND

First published in 2006 by Wayland,
an imprint of Hachette Children's Books

Copyright © Wayland 2006

Editor: Laura Milne
Managing Editor: Victoria Brooker
Senior Design Manager: Rosamund Saunders

Design: Proof Books
Commissioned photography: Chris Fairclough

Additional photography. Thanks are due to The London Fire
Brigade for kind permission to reproduce photographs: 13
(chemical suit), 15 (top), 16, 17 (top), 24, 25 (top), 26, 27.

'Be safe with the London Fire Brigade' produced and
published by the Communications Department, LFEPA
(February 2003). Illustrations by Clive Scruton.
'Like a Child to a Box of Matches' published by Home
Office Communication Directorate, 1996.
'Fire safety in the home' published by the Office of the
Deputy Prime Minister, Crown Copyright 2003.

British Library Cataloguing in Publication Data:

Thomson, Ruth
Helping hands at the fire station
1. Fire stations – Juvenile literature 2. Fire stations –
Juvenile literature
I. Title II. At the fire station
363.3'78

ISBN-10: 0-7502-4864-5
ISBN-13: 978-0-7502-4864-8

Printed and bound in China

Hachette Children's Books
A division of Hodder Headline Limited
338 Euston Road, London NW1 3BH

Acknowledgements
The author and publisher would like to thank the following
people for their help and participation in this book: Peter
Cowup, Steve Vincett, Vince Magyar and members of the
Blue Watch (Jim Burge, Dean Cooper, Simon Davis, Jim
Doherty, David Garner, Steve Green, Kelvin Jones, John
Simmonds and David Wilson) at Islington Fire Station,
London; Terry Jones, Wayne Richards, Chloe Van Dop,
Tooting Fire Station, London, and A. Hussain of London
Underground.

Contents

Words printed in **bold** are explained in the glossary.

The Blue Watch

We are firefighters. We work at a fire station.
It is open every day of the year. Four teams of
firefighters take turns to work here day and night.
Each team is called a watch.

There are ten firefighters, two crew managers and a watch manager in each watch. The watches are named after a colour – blue, green, red or white. We are the Blue Watch.

▼ The Blue Watch outside their London fire station

At the fire station

When we are on duty, we work, eat and rest at the fire station. First of all, we line up for **roll call**. Our watch manager tells us what our jobs will be in an **emergency**.

▼ The watch manager **inspects** our uniforms.

Firefighters need to be very fit. We have our own gym where we go to exercise.

We have our meals together in the canteen.

▲ The gym

▼ The canteen

The fire engine

We check both our fire engines to make sure everything is in place and working properly.

Flashing blue light to warn traffic and people that the fire engine is coming

Cab where the driver sits

Headlights

Back seats where the firefighters sit

◀ We check that every bit of **equipment** is on board the engine.

Metal ladders to reach people in tall buildings

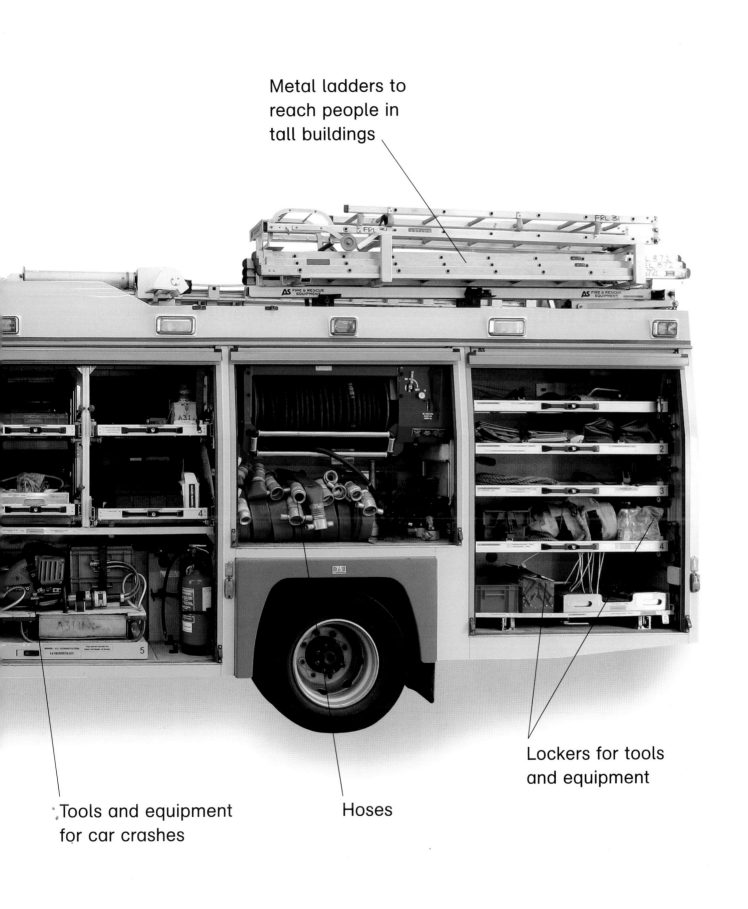

Lockers for tools and equipment

Tools and equipment for car crashes

Hoses

Tools and equipment

Fire engines carry all sorts of tools and **equipment**.

Tools for breaking open doors and windows

Crowbar

Large axe

Firefighter's axe

Bolt cutters

Fire extinguisher

Breathing apparatus helps us to breathe in places where there is smoke or poisonous gas. ▼

Equipment used for saving people from floods

A firefighter wearing an all-in-one suit, to protect him or her from harmful chemicals.▼

Lifejacket

Floating bag and line

Tools for rescuing people in car crashes

Glass saw to cut windscreens open

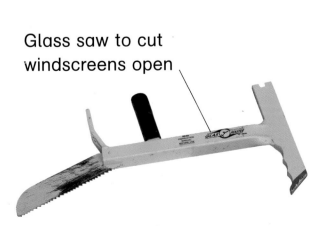

Cutters to free people from a car

Time for drill

We work on training exercises called **drills** using the high tower in the station yard.

We practise climbing up a ladder to rescue someone. ▼

▲ We lower a **dummy** from the tower instead of a real person.

We practise using a hose.

At car crashes, we may have to rescue people trapped inside. We learn how to cut the windscreen and take the roof off a car.

▼ Using cutting gear on a car

▲ The jet of water that comes out of the hose is very powerful.

Community safety

A very important part of our job is teaching people how to keep their homes safe from fire.

We fit smoke alarms and remind people to test them monthly.

▲ Smoke alarms beep loudly to warn people of fire.

◄ We hand out leaflets on fire safety.

We hold **open days** at the fire station. We tell people about fire safety.

We visit shops, schools, offices and restaurants to check they are fire safe.

Children and a firefighter at an open day ▶

▲ Discussing fire safety at the local underground station

Fire safety

∗ Never play with matches, candles, fireworks or lighters.

∗ Don't leave toys or clothes near a fire, or on top of a heater.

∗ Ask an adult to fit smoke alarms in your home.

∗ Make sure everyone in your home knows how to escape in a fire.

Firefighting uniform

When we are working at the fire station we wear t-shirts, sweatshirts and trousers. When there is an **emergency**, we put our firefighting uniform on top.

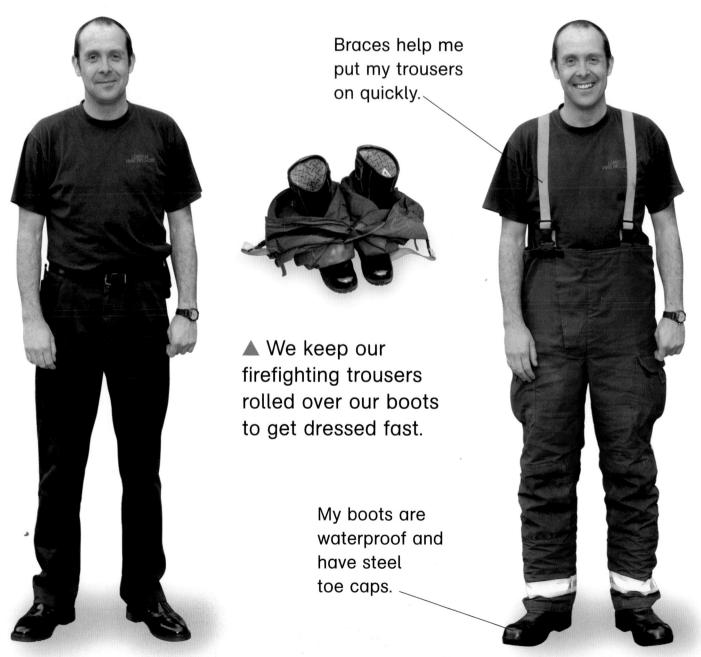

Braces help me put my trousers on quickly.

▲ We keep our firefighting trousers rolled over our boots to get dressed fast.

My boots are waterproof and have steel toe caps.

A **visor** flips down to protect my eyes.

The hard helmet protects me from falling **debris**. Its bright colour makes me easy to spot in thick smoke.

My thick jacket and trousers protect me from fire and steam.

My torch has a powerful beam.

My jacket has reflective strips.

I wear thick leather gloves.

Fire! Fire!

When there is a fire, we receive a call slip from the **control room**. It tells us about the **emergency**.

◀ We tear the call slip off the **printer**.

Sliding down the pole is quicker than using stairs. ▶

How to call the fire brigade

✳ Dial 999. The operator will ask, 'Which emergency service do you require?'

✳ Say, 'Fire.' Give your name and phone number.

✳ Say the full address and name of the nearest road. Tell the operator what you have seen.

✳ Do not put the phone down until the operator tells you to.

We also hear a message over a loudspeaker, telling us which fire engines are needed. We stop what we are doing, and slide down the pole. We put on our uniforms and climb aboard the fire engine.

▲ The driver checks where we are going on a map.

▼ On with the flashing lights and **siren**, and off we go!

Arriving at a fire

We work as a team when we arrive at a fire. We find out whether there is anyone trapped inside the building.

▲ Our watch manager tells us what to do.

◀ We fix the hose to a water **hydrant** in the street and turn on the water.

Clock

Tallies

Whistle

Radio to keep
in touch with
firefighters

◀ Tally board

Two firefighters put on their **breathing apparatus**. They give their yellow tallies to the entry control officer. He slots them into a tally board. He will be able to work out how much air they have left.

▼ The entry control officer writes down what time the firefighters go into a building.

Breathing apparatus

What to do if you discover a fire

✳ Close the door of the room where the fire is, if it is safe to do so.

✳ Get out of the building quickly by the nearest exit. Walk, don't run.

✳ Stay out. Do not go back to look for pets or toys.

✳ Call 999.

23

Putting out a fire

A burning building is very dangerous. The smoke may be thick and black. The flames are very hot. We have to stay calm and act quickly.

Firefighters always move slowly and carefully. ▶

▲ We work as a team to hose the flames.

Escaping from a fire

* Feel the door of the room you are in with the back of your hand.
* If it is cool, open it and get out.
* If there is smoke, crawl out, keeping close to the floor.
* If the door feels hot, DO NOT open it. The fire is behind it.
* Put clothes, cushions or bedding under the door to block any smoke.
* Open the window and shout, 'Fire!' Stay by the window.

Putting out a fire ▲

We put up ladders in case we need to rescue someone. We hose the flames until the fire is out. Once the fire is out, we roll up the hoses and put our equipment away.

◀ Rolling up a hose ▶

To the rescue

We also help people in other **emergencies**. We rescue people stuck in lifts or trapped by machinery. After a road accident, we may have to cut open a car to rescue a trapped driver or passenger. If a car bursts into flames, we have to put out the fire.

▲ We rescue a trapped car driver.

◄ Sometimes we rescue people caught in a flood from a burst water main.

▲ Here we are working with the Ambulance Service to rescue a man trapped down a hole.

Bury College
Woodbury LRC

Glossary

breathing apparatus the equipment that firefighters wear to give them fresh air to breathe

control room the place where all emergency calls are received and passed on to local fire stations

debris loose material (like stones) which could be dangerous

drills the training exercises that firefighters use to practise for an emergency

dummy a stuffed model of a person that firefighters use for rescue practice

emergency a sudden dangerous event, such as a fire, flood or car crash, which needs instant action

equipment tools and other things that people use for their job

fire extinguisher hand-held equipment that can quickly put out small fires

hydrant an underground pipe which supplies water for fire engines

inspect look at closely

open day a day for the public to visit a place

printer a machine that prints out messages from the Fire Brigade's control room

roll call calling out names of the firefighters on duty to make sure everyone is there

siren a horn that makes a loud warning noise on fire engines and other emergency vehicles

visor a movable part of a helmet covering the face

Quiz

Look back through the book to do this quiz.

1 What telephone number should you dial if there is a fire?

2 What is a firefighting team called?

3 What uniform does a firefighter put on for firefighting?

4 What equipment do firefighters wear if they think the air is not safe to breathe?

5 What should all homes have fitted for fire safety?

6 How often should you test your smoke alarm?

7 Where do firefighters get water from to put out a fire?

8 Why does a fire engine use a siren and flashing lights?

Answers

1 999
2 A watch
3 Jacket, trousers, boots, gloves and helmet
4 Breathing apparatus
5 A smoke alarm
6 Once a month
7 A water hydrant
8 To warn people and traffic of the fire engine

Useful contacts

www.london-fire.gov.uk
The website of the London Fire Brigade. Go to the schools and children section for fire safety information for teachers and pupils. It also provides information on the London Fire Brigade's Juvenile Fire Setters Intervention Scheme, and LIFE (Local Intervention Fire Education programme).

Places to visit

Visit the London Fire Brigade Museum and see how firefighting has developed over the last 340 years. Book your visit by contacting:

London Fire Brigade Museum, Winchester House, 94a Southwark Bridge Road, London SE1 0EG. Tel: 020 7587 2894

Firefighting work can be dangerous, tiring and dirty, but we wouldn't swap it for any other job.

Index